P9-AOY-224

The Hard Work
of Simple Living

The Hard Work of Simple Living

A Somewhat Blank Book for the Sustainable Hedonist

Artwork by Edward Koren

with contributions
from the Invisible Universe

Chelsea Green Publishing Company   White River Junction, Vermont

Copyright 1998 Chelsea Green Publishing Company.
Cartoons copyright 1998 Edward Koren.

Permission has generously been granted for the use of cartoons by Edward Koren
previously published in *The New Yorker*.

All rights reserved. No part of this book may be transmitted in any form by any means
without permission in writing from the publisher.

Printed in Canada.
First printing, September 1998.

01 00 99 98   1 2 3 4 5

This book is printed on acid-free and recycled paper.
Cataloging-in-Publication Data appears at the end of the book.

Designed by Ann Aspell.

Edited by Rachael Cohen.

Chelsea Green Publishing Company
Post Office Box 428
White River Junction, VT 05001
(800) 639-4099
http://www.chelseagreen.com

Foreword

A decade ago, when I was poring over the early data on global warming for a book I was writing called *The End of Nature,* it became clear to me that We Are Going To Have To Change The Way We Live. That's what I told my readers, and that's what I told myself. But change is harder than it seems—the inertia of our lives is strong, and stronger still is the seductive power of the consumer world into which we are born.

It gradually dawned on me that we were not going to make fundamental shifts in our lives simply for fear that we would wreck the planet. We weren't going to ride bikes in order to reduce our emissions of carbon dioxide. But we might ride bikes if we decided they were more *fun than driving*—fun because you can see the world at a friendly pace, fun because you feel your muscles and your lungs working the way they're supposed to work, fun because a few months of biking makes you stronger, fitter, *sexier.* And thus was born what this book delightfully calls a "sustainable hedonist." Someone who likes organic, close-to-home apple cider because it tastes so good, someone who wants local vegetables from farmer neighbors because they're full of flavor. Someone who sometimes turns off the lights at night not merely to save energy but because he likes candlelight.

This book makes evident just how useful Chelsea Green Publishing Company has been in the development of the skills necessary for this subtle revolution. Many of the books and authors have been on my shelf for years, often consulted: Michael Phillips, Gene Logsdon, Eliot Coleman, the Nearings, and many, many others. Though their subject is "simple" living, much of the advice proffered is reasonably difficult. This way of life is harder than the typical suburban life. But the pleasure comes at least as much in the *doing*—pruning trees, digging vegetable beds, building a home—as in the ultimate results.

If there is any trap that "simple livers" must avoid at all costs, it is sanctimony. Hence, Edward Koren's wonderful and gentle jabs, aimed equally at the status quo and at the Vermont alternative orthodoxy. Ed is simply the funniest cartoonist in America, and has been for many years. And he provides an invaluable inoculation against solemnity and self-righteousness. For if I have figured out anything about our consumer society, it is this: fear and guilt and even reason are feeble weapons with which to fight it. The only genuinely subversive thing you can do in America is have more fun than other people. Which is not so hard. So get to it.

Bill McKibben

Introduction

"Simple living" is hot. And, as with any hot topic, you can hear the publishers stampeding to jump on the bandwagon. When the dust clears, simple living will have been scrutinized from every imaginable angle. A succession of gurus will hawk their wares on Imus and Oprah. There will be simple living for dummies, simple living from Mars and Venus, and simple living for the soul.

We live simply at Chelsea Green, and we publish books that help folks live simply. We do not, however, publish "simple living" books, for the "simple" reason that our experience has taught us that real simple living is hard work.

It's hard work to power your home with solar electricity; it's hard work to garden organically instead of with chemical fertilizers; it's hard work to heat your home with wood; and it's hard work to question the big assumptions instead of following the beaten path.

The "simple living" phenomenon can be traced to Thoreau in the United States, and back to ancient philosophers in the Old World who sang the praises of pastoral life. The most prominent recent practitioners were Scott and Helen Nearing, who developed an independent homestead called Forest Farm on a beautiful site on the coast of Maine. The Nearings built their spectacular home of stone using rocks gathered from the nearby beach. Perhaps most remarkably, they began their construction project when Helen was in her seventies and Scott was in his nineties. They described their circumstances as "the good life," because they found the hard work to be balanced by many rewards.

Among the many people to be inspired by the Nearings were Ian and Margo Baldwin, founders of Chelsea Green. They were not seventy and ninety when they started their small publishing company on the village green in the tiny town of Chelsea, Vermont, but they knew that their road to prosperity would be steep and muddy. It would be hard work, but worth the effort.

Among their rewards is the fact that Chelsea Green is now the official publishing partner for the Good Life Center, the estate of Scott and Helen Nearing.

Other Nearing disciples have gone on to write books for Chelsea Green. Eliot Coleman took the Nearings' model of chemical-free gardening and showed how it could be the foundation of a small-scale business, in *The New Organic Grower.* He has now developed methods for growing fresh vegetables year-round, even in northern New England, as described in *Four-Season Harvest.* It's hard work, but nothing tastes as good, or makes us feel as good, as home-grown organic produce, right from the garden.

Today, at the dawn of the New Millennium, the Nearings are still inspiring people to live independent lives, but this process is now unfolding with surprising and delightful nuances. The "good life," as a practice, is more relevant than ever. Its practitioners are found worldwide and express a dazzling variety of lifeways. They are building straw bale houses in southern Arizona and passive solar houses in Vermont. They are the masonry-hearth bread bakers of Marin County, and the enlightened woodlot managers on Wisconsin tree farms. They are conservation-minded suburbanites in northern New Jersey, and flower farmers in Kansas. They are the seekers of green lanes in England, and the solar pioneers of Gaviotas in Colombia. They are the contrary farmers of Ohio, and the sauna builders of northeastern New York.

They are multitudinous and they are everywhere, and they are all denizens of what Ian Baldwin calls "The Invisible Universe."

What name do we give to these practical, playful, realistic idealists? In our culture of labels and sound bites, a group that defies categorization must surely be illegal. Yet we can describe them: They appreciate and emulate nature, and don't hog all the resources for themselves. They want to live comfortably, safely, and well, and they are not afraid to have a rollicking good time doing it. They laugh as much as they can.

Michael Potts uses the term "sustainable hedonist" to describe the Pomo Indians, the original inhabitants of the coastal ridges of northern California where he lives. Michael, a dyed-in-the-wool resident of The Invisible Universe, has studied and chronicled the contemporary practices of homesteading in his books *The Independent Home* and its newly revised edition, *The New Independent Home.* The energy pioneers he portrays live mostly off-the-grid, free from utility-generated electricity, in innovative shelters of their own design. These folks, more enchanting than Spartan, are indulgent in their applications of technology yet consummately conscious of the impact of their actions upon the environment.

The Pomo, says Michael, embraced technology through their basket making. He compares this "gentle organizational tool" with its modern counterpart, the plastic container. The creation of the latter is possible only with the consumption of vast amounts of fossil-fuel energy, using processes that are extractive, exploitative, and above all, wasteful. The result is inferior in almost every way.

> A new basket grows organically in our hands: we bend and weave wet reeds with our clever hands, and order emerges. The shapes are curved, human, pleasing, the texture benign and familiar. There is much room for practice and for art. A well-woven basket made from the right stuff holds water, and can be used for cooking. With only slight changes in material and technique, this flexible technology, weaving, can produce clothing, shelter, games . . . all the essential human necessities and delights. The finished work is pleasing beyond any mechanistic definition of function, conferring on maker and user alike a heightened sense of participation in the planet's greater web of life.*

Now, compare that to the pleasure you get buying the plastic container down at Mega-Discount-Plus-Mart.

The Pomo, according to Potts, were archetypal sustainable hedonists. The same moniker would fit Michael himself. He lives on a promontory that overlooks the Pacific much the way that Forest Farm overlooks Penobscot Bay (except the ocean is on the wrong side!). He lives a West Coast version of the good life, harvesting electrons from the Sun so that he can "work hard" as a computer consultant and webmaster, pursuits that provide a more reliable income stream than that of an author. It's a lifestyle that expresses particularly eloquently the true potential of homesteading in America in the late twentieth century.

Michael agreed to loan us his concept of the "sustainable hedonist" for this book project. We think it describes the only club in which all of us at Chelsea Green would like to be members. This is a group that defies demographics and includes all ages, sexes, religions, and nationalities. Its members share a set of values that articulate basic relationships between the human race and the planet. The underlying concept is powerful in its utter simplicity.

To help us create this book, we turned to cartoonist Edward Koren, whose values are embedded in both his art and his way of life. He, too, overlooks a body of water from his home, albeit a small, freshwater pond crossed by a

---

*Learn more about sustainable hedonism, the Pomo Indians, and solar energy on Michael Potts's website < www.solarnet.org > .

floating bridge in Pond Village, which, as you all know, is a kind of suburb of Brookfield, Vermont (population 483). His characters are often drawn from the urban and suburban world, and his captions are slices of insight that point out the ironies of how we live. I imagine his work, like the basket making of the Pomo, brings rich rewards to the creator, as to the consumer. His touch, deft and unmistakable, is that of a sustainable hedonist.

My personal connection with Ed comes from the times we have traversed the Vermont landscape together, usually on bicycles or cross-country skis. We gossip about shared acquaintances, local politics, and small-town stuff. Occasionally, his beeper goes off: Ed is a volunteer fireman. As an artist whose work is published frequently in *The New Yorker,* he is clearly from a different world than the rest of the fire department, most of whom wouldn't be caught dead with a subscription to such a "flatlander" publication (but who peek at the cartoons in the dentist office). I venture that his fellow fire fighters scratch their heads when they think of what Ed does in his studio each day. And I'll bet more than once he has been greeted with "Workin' hard? Or hardly workin'?"

The other main ingredients of the book are contributions from around The Invisible Universe: quotations from the books of Chelsea Green's authors and distributed publishers.

We invite you to complete this "somewhat blank" book yourself. Fill the pages with your own words, sketches, scribbles, thoughts, stories, and memories. Paste in images snipped from elsewhere; map your backyard; plan your garden; list the books you'll read next summer; brainstorm your next building project; write a poem. You too can be a certifiable "sustainable hedonist" and book-toting denizen of The Invisible Universe. With your help, we can create the greatest story ever told.

Stephen Morris
President & Publisher
Chelsea Green Publishing Company
White River Junction, Vermont, and Totnes, England

"Today, we examined our life style, we evaluated our diet and our exercise program, and we also assessed our behavioral patterns. Then we felt we needed a drink."

"People who dare to build a utopia use the same materials available to anyone, but they find surprising ways to combine them."

Gustavo Yepes, quoted in Alan Weisman, *Gaviotas*

♦

"My work is to stare into space."

Visioning means imagining, at first generally and then with increasing specificity, what you really want. That is *what you really want,* not what someone has taught you to want, and not what you have learned to be willing to settle for. Visioning means taking off all the constraints of assumed "feasibility," of disbelief and past disappointments, and letting your mind dwell upon its most noble, uplifting, treasured dreams.

♦ Donella H. Meadows, Dennis L. Meadows, and Jørgen Randers, *Beyond the Limits*

It's often easier and more productive
to widen a window of opportunity
than to build a whole new door.

Nancy Cole and P. J. Skerrett, ♦
Renewables Are Ready

"Be gentle with it, men. It's a historic landmark."

"Is there anyone here who specializes in stress management?"

The fact is,
compared to
pigs, we humans
are unforgivably
slow to learn
from pragmatic
experience.

Karl Schwenke, ◆
In a Pig's Eye

"I am always happy in spring digging out rocks and stones
to build something with."

John Burroughs, from a letter to Clara Barrus (3 April 1902),
quoted in Edward J. Renehan, Jr.,
John Burroughs

♦

"Your work must be very satisfying."

"Ah—the celestial Mozart!"

Artistry can also be in the honesty
of one's lifestyle, in one's order, in one's character. . . .
Scott was an artist in his neat and tidy, thriving vegetable gardens,
in his straight wood and compost piles, in his brightly shining tools,
in his meticulous notebooks, in his careful, legible script.
I felt he made his very life a work of art.

Helen Nearing,
Loving and Leaving the Good Life

♦

At this moment I do not
follow the distinction
between managed and
unmanaged joy, between
trees and hardware stores,
between sunsets and a
gorgeous chisel that
balances perfectly in the
palm of your hand, the
steel blade reaching out like
the edge of a canyon, hawk
sharp, to cut into wood, the
handle of the chisel fitting
so well you can hold it and
instantly know how good
everything is.

♦ Thomas Glynn,
Hammer. Nail. Wood.

"Hugh understands wood."

"It's fairly straightforward. Just figure out how to build the future of civilization from grass, sun, and water."

♦ Jorge Zapp, quoted in Alan Weisman, *Gaviotas*

"Could you fellas tell me if there's anyplace around here where I could find a fax machine?"

Society praises as science and art the ability to swing a ball bat, golf club, or tennis racket skillfully. If we would expend a fraction of that kind of attention and honor on the hoe, ax, shovel, and pitchfork, we might be surprised about how much work that humans could accomplish.

♦ Gene Logsdon, *The Contrary Farmer*

"Well, it has been a great summer for chanterelles."

If you asked, "How do I flush a toilet, where does it go?" a professional would say, "You have a septic tank, you have a leaching field, it's this big." That's the end of the professional response. But I may look at that and say, "No, there are other ways to do this that make more sense."

♦ William McDonough, "Reviving the Ancient Art of Design," in Chris Zelov and Phil Cousineau, editors, *Design Outlaws on the Ecological Frontier*

"The majority will always be for caution, hesitation, and the status quo—always against creation and innovation. The innovator—he who leaves the beaten track—must therefore always be a minoritarian—always be an object of opposition, scorn, hatred. It is part of the price he must pay for the ecstasy that accompanies creative thinking and acting."

♦ Scott Nearing, quoted from his papers in Helen Nearing, *Loving and Leaving the Good Life*

"Go straight until you get to the Body Shop. Then there's a path to the right that leads to the Gap. A little farther along, just past the Limited, there's a clearing. Victoria's Secret is right there."

Fruits, flowers, and vegetables all thrive in
fertile soil—loose and well-drained—where
roots can easily absorb vital nutrients. Plants
need exposure to the proper amount of sunlight,
air circulation, and an ample supply of water. A
house must be planted in the right type of soil
as well: firm for good bearing, yet well-drained
for a solid foundation.

♦ David Easton, *The Rammed Earth House*

"Made with pride in our basement."

Julian designed the new house himself.
In doing so, he used the uncomfortable,
inconvenient, and inefficient home his
father built thirty years before
as a reverse model.

Edward J. Renehan, Jr.,
John Burroughs

♦

"Please help us reduce our garbage and improve our energy efficiency and our water quality. Help us to be eco-wise and— above all—to empower others."

Today I am older, wiser, and more patient—
not a saint, mind you, but I mulch with the dedication of a champion chess player
and the fervent sincerity of a young priest.

Ron L. Engeland, *Growing Great Garlic*

♦

KOREN

I believe in a simple law and corollary. The law states, "There is always a way." The corollary states, "Once you find a way, there is always a better way."

Eliot Coleman, *The New Organic Grower* ♦

The contrary farmer also enjoys hard work out of a sort of mule-headed stoicism. I like getting hot, tired, and dirty putting up hay because it feels so good to clean up in the evening, sit on the porch, and sip lemonade, especially if it is spiked with gin.

♦ Gene Logsdon, *The Contrary Farmer*

"I work four hours in the morning. Then meditation and errands."

"I've <u>done</u> my tour of duty on Wall Street."

With us contrary farmers rests a holy possibility. Our so-called "economy" has no place in it for enterprises that will pay off only twenty, forty, or sixty years from now, or not at all. Only those who have found a way to extricate their lives, or at least a little part of their lives, from the enslavement of that economy can "afford" to plant groves of trees instead of corn and cotton.

Gene Logsdon, *The Contrary Farmer* ◆

What?

You don't
smoke, you
don't drink,
you don't have
expensive toys,
you don't run
around with
the neighbor's
spouse?
You are
disadvantaged.
You are, as
Mark Twain
said, "like a
sinking ship
with no freight
to throw
overboard."

♦ Rob Roy,
Mortgage-Free!

"Reassess our life style? Why?"

"Do you ever miss New York?"

"It's awfully hard to explain to someone, you come home at night, say someone's there dropped by for a visit, you come in the door and your clothes are all torn up, there's blood dripping off your nose where you banged it on something, you're tired, you're hunched over because your back hurts . . ." Jimmy Moffatt laughs and shakes his head. "It's awfully hard to explain to that person that Yes, this is the way it is, but Gee I had a good time today."

Tree farmer Jim Moffatt, in David Dobbs and Richard Ober, *The Northern Forest* ◆

We saw our good life not as a model for others but as a pilgrimage, for us, to the best way we could conceive of living. We felt a glad responsibility in joining with the stream of onward life, with the whole magnificent enterprise. This was living a life of affirmation, of contribution, of making every act and every day purposeful. To live the good life, we found, was to do the best we were capable of in any set of circumstances.

♦ Helen Nearing, *Loving and Leaving the Good Life*

It's a great way of life, woods work.

You can always make ten dollars as long as you're willing to spend eleven.
Anybody that wants to log can barely make it till they die.
But it's a great way of life.

Larry Moffatt, logger, in David Dobbs and Richard Ober, *The Northern Forest*

♦

"Happy?"

He lived, not in a cabin, but in a real house built of stone that bore plain evidence of how his own efforts had reclaimed the ruin he had found there on his arrival. His roof was strong and sound. The wind on its tiles made the sound of the sea upon its shore.

♦ Jean Giono, *The Man Who Planted Trees*

"It was obviously built when the Mayans were feeling good about themselves."

A house isn't so precious. It should have a roof that doesn't leak, or hardly leaks. It should be reasonably warm. Some windows to let in the sun and air when and where you want them would be nice and also to keep them out when you don't. The windows should give good views. They should be reasonably large, reasonably efficient. It doesn't make too much difference where the living room, dining room, or kitchen is. They can be the same room. A few bedrooms, upstairs. A bathroom. Water. Plumbing. Electricity. Maybe a cellar, maybe not. A porch, yes.

♦ Thomas Glynn, *Hammer. Nail. Wood.*

There's no feeling like the feeling of security you get when the wind is howling and torrential rain or sleet or ice is beating down upon the earth and pummeling one's house, and a stone roof stands guard overhead deflecting mother nature's blows.

Joseph Jenkins, *The Slate Roof Bible* ♦

Comfort, like beauty,
is its own excuse for being,
but it has a practical function,
too, because comfort is
essential to safety.

♦ Robert Kimber,
A Canoeist's Sketchbook

"I'm in here—luxuriating."

"Isn't this <u>fun</u>?"

I came to farming from an adventuring background. I was a passionate rock climber, mountaineer, and whitewater kayaker. Organic farming appealed to me because it involved searching for and discovering nature's pathways, as opposed to the formulaic approach of chemical farming. The appeal of organic farming is boundless; this mountain has no top, this river has no end. Every day I delight in the continuing adventure.

Eliot Coleman, *The New Organic Grower* ♦

The breaks we take on gravel bars or maple-bestudded points are, ostensibly, utilitarian. We stop to eat, to stretch our legs, to catch forty winks and recharge our batteries, but we also take them to see much of what we've come here to see, to hear what we've come to hear. Out on the water, we live in the large dimensions. Here on the gravel bar is where we make friends with the moth and the inchworm. Here, where we stretch out in the noonday sun and sweet torpor starts to overtake us, is where we truly have our ears to the ground . . .

♦ Robert Kimber, *A Canoeist's Sketchbook*

"I love this planet!"

"It's very sensitive of you to realize that men <u>like</u> to get flowers!"

One day
even human beings,
intent on destroying
the environment on
which they depend,
and absorbed in
their own narrow,
greedy aims, will
discover that beauty
is a biological
necessity.

Robert Hart, ♦
Forest Gardening

There is nothing more real in this life than land. Earth gives us each thing we have, and at the end we return those gifts to it. "Owning land" is a relatively modern notion and by no means a universal practice. In fact, to many of the world's peoples who live intimately with the land, the idea of ownership is incomprehensible. The search for good land is like the search for a mate. We certainly hope to find sustenance, partnership, comfort, and stability. In the end, if we truly wish to settle peacefully and productively, we must find love and passion for the land as well.

♦ Michael Potts, in *Real Goods Solar Living Sourcebook*

"It's a beautiful country, all right—if you can afford it."

More people are going to need to be involved in farming again, whether directly on the land or engaged in an interactive economy that makes neighborly farming possible. This is a good thing. So many imponderables get answered when we turn from the *big and naughty* to the *small and beautiful.*

Michael Phillips, ◆
The Apple Grower

The negative image many
people carry of "salesmen"
stems from the association
of that profession with
unwanted, unneeded, shoddy,
poorly made, frivolous
products that require fast
talking and other unsavory
skills to sell. Good growers
should understand that they
are not in the same
category at all.

Eliot Coleman,
The New Organic Grower

◆

"Sure, this is idyllic, but there are fundamental problems here that are not being addressed."

Ironically enough,
the more one
immerses oneself in
the complexity of the
familiar, the more one
can attain simplicity of
life. We contrary
gardeners often refer
to this simplicity as
"the simple life," even
though we know that
its manifestations are
simple only by very
complex design.

Gene Logsdon, ♦
The Contrary Farmer's
Invitation to Gardening

Living the good life for us was practicing harmony with the earth and all that lives on it. It was frugal living, self-subsistent, self-sustaining. It was earning our way by the sweat of our brows, beholden to no employer or job. It was growing our own food, building our own buildings, cutting our own wood, and providing for our own livelihood. We needed and used little money. If we couldn't pay for a thing, we made it ourselves or did without.

♦ Helen Nearing, *Loving and Leaving the Good Life*

"We motored over to say hi!"

For me and for many other men and women who appreciate some level of energy independency, there is an honor and an honesty to the time taken on system maintenance. It reveals my ambivalence about the automobile that I will not assume responsibility for its vile underside; I am in no way ambivalent about caring for my home power system, which presents a clean, appropriate, understandable, and rewarding challenge. Its diverse parts work so well, and are so easy to keep running, that I need only remember to give each component the small quantum of attention it requires.

♦ Michael Potts, *The Independent Home*

"Have you given any thought to what you'll do with your Saturdays when the world's fossil fuels are used up?"

Solar energy can help bring back that taste of happiness

that people feel when they control their own resources and their community's economic destiny.

♦ Daniel M. Berman and John T. O'Connor, *Who Owns the Sun?*

Former tribal chair
Abbot Sekaquaptewa once compared
photovoltaics to farming: "It's the same principle
as when you raise corn and you gather the fruit of the earth.
You're nursing from your mother." Many Hopis demonstrate this
connection by offering prayer feathers to their photovoltaic panels,
just as they do to their crops, rivers, the sun, and the earth.

Nancy Cole and P. J. Skerrett, *Renewables Are Ready*

♦

Every electrician knows the feeling:

You are about to throw "the switch." You turn your head away, close the only two eyes you own, grit your teeth, and commit the circuit! More often than we like to admit, all hell breaks loose. I initiated this [grid-photovoltaic] tie-in with the push of a button. There was a deafening silence, beautiful and wonderful in a way that only an electrician could understand. Nothing blew up or even groaned or sparked. The utility meter just began to slow and then to spin backwards. Solar poetry in motion.

♦ Jeff Oldham, project manager, in John Schaeffer et al.,
A Place in the Sun

"I hear you enjoy tinkering."

"I don't own a wood stove. I burn oil."

The eternal light shining through a Star of David sculpture above Temple Emanuel's ark uses no utility power, no oil, or candles. But it's no miracle either—two 9-by-13-inch solar panels on the temple's roof feed electricity to two 6-volt industrial storage batteries, which power the light. . . . It's a perfect match between energy source and application, says Rabbi Everett Gendler.

Nancy Cole and
P. J. Skerrett,
*Renewables
Are Ready*

If we can put men on the moon, if we can splice genes, we certainly ought to be able to design neighborhoods that are energy efficient and have a sense of community, much like the communities that existed prior to the advent of the automobile.

♦ Mike Corbett, "Why Can't We Build Better Communities?," in Chris Zelov and Phil Cousineau, editors, *Design Outlaws on the Ecological Frontier*

"Call off the siege. It's being converted into ninety-three units of cooperative housing."

"I've just bought five acres of prime oceanfront. Want to help me build on it?"

We would come together as a family to build.

There was never a right or wrong way—we just did it however
we knew how. We used whatever was close by: rocks from the wash,
dirt from the side of the house, or the neighbor's melting adobe blocks.
The process was not much different from making pottery and bread, and
primarily involved women and children. Little ones learned as they played
alongside us. Our hands coated with mud, we would let the earth take form and
watch with amazement as it did. We would laugh at each other and at ourselves.

Athena Swentzell Steen, in *The Straw Bale House* ♦

"Our goal is to modernize it but retain the historical flavor."

So imagine that one day within the next ten years, you wake up in a house whose walls, roof, flooring, insulation, and paint are derived from hemp. You feel great after sleeping on your hemp-stuffed mattress, covered with soft linens spun from hemp fiber. Your feet sink into the hemp carpeting as you get out of bed and open the hemp drapes. It's a beautiful morning.

John W. Roulac, *Hemp Horizons* ♦

Junk cars are a classic example of recycling.

For many they are a source of economic security. They are used for spare parts for the car that does run. They also make useful outbuildings in which to store tools and equipment and other stuff that someday you might need. They are good for sitting on in the evening while talking to a neighbor. They make handy chicken coops. They protect grain bags from the rain. They are great for kids to play around— perfect for hide-and-seek.

Frank Bryan and John McClaughry,
The Vermont Papers: Recreating Democracy on a Human Scale

♦

"We sing her to sleep with songs about recycling."

While I'd like to build the perfect house, it makes more sense to me to design and build the pretty efficient, largely non-toxic, mildly recycled, partially timbered, semi-great house. It will not only cost less, but wear better than a more innovative or radical design, or a more literal interpretation of a design philosophy.

♦ Sam Clark, *The Real Goods Independent Builder*

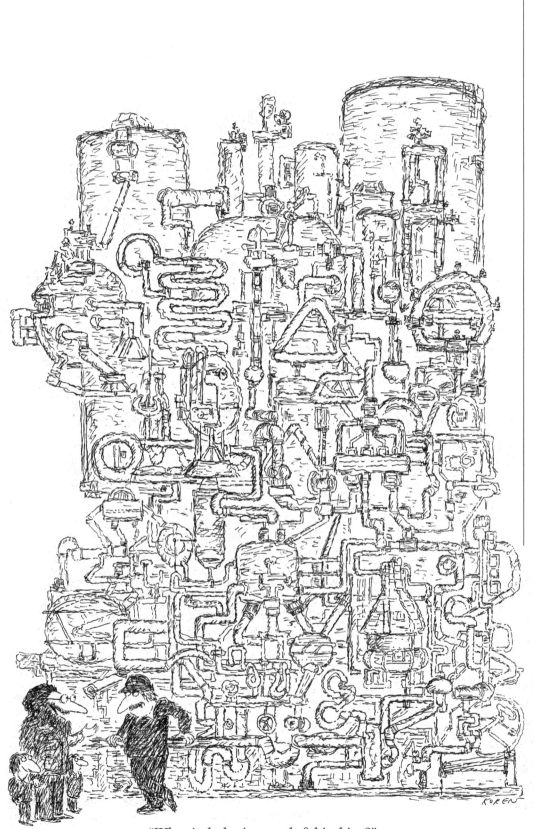

"Where's the business end of this thing?"

I know my limitations and will not presume that I can any more break through an
unbelieving spirit with facts and figures than that a preacher can break through a
hard heart with the love of the gospel. Our hearts define what our minds will believe.

♦ Joel Salatin, *Salad Bar Beef*

"I think Jules is reminding Nat that each and every one of us produces four pounds of garbage each day, every day."

Composting is easier to do than to describe,
and, like lovemaking, magic when you do it well.

Sim Van der Ryn, *The Toilet Papers*

♦

For poison ivy, one remedy was to rub the inside of a ripe banana peel on the itchy area and, of course, eat the banana if you like.

Emma Byler (Jonas Em), *Plain & Happy Living* ◆

I will never forget the day I introduced my mother to my composting system. . .

"Smell this," I said. So she put her nose right up to the black earth I held out before me and took a deep breath.

"Boy, that smells good!" she said, inhaling the rich, sweet-smelling aroma of fertile soil, and smiling.

"This is my alternative to a septic system!" I proudly informed her, still holding the compost out in front of me as I watched her smile suddenly freeze.

♦ Joseph Jenkins,
The Humanure Handbook

"I certainly hope you're composting the leftovers."

KOREN

Going into a strange kitchen
I often have the urge to check out the
garbage pail. Finding it filled with fruit
peelings, spoiled leftovers, yesterday's
newspaper, beer cans, glass jars, steak
bones, and plastic wrapping brings
me to find my hosts and deliver
a composting lecture.

Sim Van der Ryn, ♦
The Toilet Papers

In China and Japan, "night soil" has been scrupulously collected for centuries to fertilize the fields. . . . Farmers vied with each other to build the most beautiful roadside privies in hopes of attracting the favors of travelers who needed to relieve themselves.

Sim Van der Ryn, *The Toilet Papers* ◆

During my visit, I had to be content with a privy for a bathroom, but that proved to be a pleasant interlude, too. As I sat there, I became aware of a wren in a nest on the wall beside me. Mother Wren stared at me, but did not move. I felt that I should talk to her, but could think of nothing that might interest a wren.

♦ Gene Logsdon, *The Contrary Farmer's Invitation to Gardening*

I think my own view of wealth is also love. One of the errors that economists and a lot of futurists make is that they think that somehow human beings, because they are so clever, can get cleverer, and cleverer, and opt out of having to do any physical work themselves. The problem with that is that there is, as all women in the world know, an irreducible amount of physical effort that goes into nurturing the next generation. There is no way you can delegate changing a baby's diaper.

♦ Hazel Henderson, "Redefining Wealth," in Chris Zelov and Phil Cousineau, editors, *Design Outlaws on the Ecological Frontier*

MEN
DRINKING
COFFEE

KOREN.

If we choose to live beyond the fringes of powerlines without living like troglodytes, we must become our own little power companies and take responsibility for the whole electric enterprise: generating and storing it; transmitting it from source to demand; and distributing it among the loads, where it sheds light, performs work, amuses and instructs us, and powers all the myriad uses we have created in this electricity-infatuated era. Suppliers as well as consumers, off-the-gridders quickly come to grips with the finite energy budget within which we all must learn to live comfortably.

♦ Michael Potts, in *Real Goods Solar Living Sourcebook*

"I'm never bored! I've got my pottery, my plants, my weaving, and my man."

What might appear to be objective physical misery

coexisting with the greatest subjective glee constitutes an oxymoron too,
and perhaps goes to show that it takes a moron to appreciate an oxymoron.

♦ Robert Kimber, *A Canoeist's Sketchbook*

"While you've been out tormenting your bodies, I've been enjoying an active and satisfying gastric life."

The human animal's use of sunlight is indirect. We can't photosynthesize, so we consume vast amounts of stored sunlight as food. Within our bodies, the sunlight is combusted in a process remarkably similar to what happens to a stick of wood in a fire. The resulting conversion process creates warmth and energy.

♦ Stephen Morris, in John Schaeffer et al., *A Place in the Sun*

"I'm tired of food."

"I love this place—its food, its ambience, and its political goals."

The only really good advice that holds up in all situations is:
Always make friends with the cook.

Gene Logsdon, *The Contrary Farmer*

♦

"I don't feel like going out. Why don't just the two of us stay in and open a can of worms?"

Some ants heat their colony by taking turns sitting out in the sun soaking up its radiant heat and then going back inside to act as living portable heaters.

John S. Taylor, *A Shelter Sketchbook* ♦

Nature is a vast killing
field. No bug, plant, or
animal including
humans can live unless
other bugs, plants, or
animals die. All we do is
trade corporeal forms
around the gaming table
of existential matter.

◆ Gene Logsdon,
   The Contrary Farmer

"You hate to shop—I hate to hunt."

We live in a world that has practiced violence
for generations—violence to other creatures, violence to the planet, violence
to ourselves. Yet in my garden, where I have nurtured a healthy soil-plant
community, I see a model of a highly successful, non-violent system where
I participate in gentle biological diplomacy rather
than war. The garden has more to
teach us than just how to grow food.

Eliot Coleman, *Four-Season Harvest*

♦

"I think this may be an appropriate moment to say a few words in memory of the animals we've slaughtered for our pleasure."

Sensual and spiritual,

symbol of both simplicity and transcendent mystery,
bread rewards the baker in each step of its creation but achieves
its true purpose only when broken and shared. This vehicle of life
then becomes, somehow, us, and the cycle continues.

John McLure, *Baba À Louis Bakery Bread Book*

♦

"Food as metaphor for love? Again?"

Chili peppers refuse to be tamed,
codified, classified, and otherwise put in their
place. Adventurous and spirited, they mix
and match, reproduce unpredictably and
prolifically, and generally run their own show.

♦ Dianne Onstad, *Whole Foods Companion*

"I'm beginning to think it's salsa that's causing your mood swings."

"Joel! Killer crust!"

The making of bread is elemental—calling for earth, air, fire, and water in the right proportion and in nature's time. In the meeting of earth, as present in broken grain, and spirit, as expressed through the hands of the baker, bread becomes the balancing point of life for the person with eyes to see.

Peter Farrar, in John McLure, ♦
Baba À Louis Bakery Bread Book

The aroma
of cinnamon has
also proven to be an
aphrodisiac in a
recent study . . .
in which male
subjects sniffed a
variety of odors.
Freshly baked
cinnamon rolls
scored the highest
response of the ten
odors tested.

Dianne Onstad,
*Whole Foods
Companion*

♦

"How about a kiss?"

We regard pigs as a learning experience.

♦ Karl Schwenke, *In a Pig's Eye*

It's pretty hard to be dishonest
when you are totally naked.

Rob Roy, *The Sauna*

♦

Scott and I had our yeasty moments together. One warm spring day we had been skiing in shorts on an isolated hill on the Fern Pass in Tirolese, Austria. I proposed taking off everything, so, nude, we sped down the slopes wearing only big ski boots and skis. What a sight that would have been for onlookers.

Helen Nearing, ♦
Loving and Leaving
the Good Life

"One experiences everything quite differently when one is warm than when one is cold."

♦ Edvard Munch, quoted in Bente Torjusen, editor, *Words and Images of Edvard Munch*

SOON
TO BE
A
SWEATER

KOREN

Will the sauna cause pregnancy? Not likely.

Rob Roy, *The Sauna*

♦

"We've decided not to have children."

Growing old

is living on the descending
arc of the cycle of life between
earth and death. It has many advantages
as well as the obvious disadvantages of diminishing
physical capacities. One is over the hump; one has done
more or less what one could; not much is expected any more.

♦ Helen Nearing, *Loving and Leaving the Good Life*

"I'm just getting around to sowing my wild oats."

"He who plants a coconut tree plants food and drink, vessels and clothing, a habitation for himself, and a heritage for his children."

South Sea proverb, quoted in Dianne Onstad, *Whole Foods Companion*

"According to this, everything we've done up to now is right."

The beauty of birds and butterflies, moths and dragonflies feeds the human soul as much as fruit, nuts, and herbs feed the human body. I shall never forget the sudden revelation, in the summer of 1989, of coming upon the deep purple buddleia on the rose mound in the arboretum, teeming with a multitude of many-colored butterflies. No scene in a tropical forest could have been more beautiful. It was an experience of a lifetime, a reward for years of hard labor.

♦ Robert Hart, *Forest Gardening*

"What beautiful asparagus!"

Although it takes me two hours to mow the lawn, I now know it could be much worse. If I had to mow the original North American prairie, more than one million square miles of grass, it would take me about nine million years working eight hours a day. If I volunteered to also take care of the desert grasslands of the Southwest, the Palouse prairie of southeastern Washington, and the interior grasslands of California, all isolated mature grasslands, I would be busy for another million years. Fortunately, other arrangements were made for maintaining the grasslands: drought.

♦ Ted Levin, *Blood Brook*

While most Americans
are spending millions
to eradicate dandelions
from their yards, other
Americans are buying
dandelion seeds from
Nichols, Stokes, the
Cook's Garden, and
other seed houses.

Peter Gail, ♦
The Dandelion Celebration

The best part of mowing and collecting forage for composting is the lack of concern about weather. Anyone who has ever struggled to make hay in an uncooperative climate will appreciate this new, relaxed attitude. Instead of worrying about the hay crop being rained on, I look forward to it. Instead of carefully setting the hayrake to just skim the surface, I intentionally set it too deep so it will kick soil and old thatch into the new mowings. All the practices that would be negatives if I were striving to make hay for feeding four-legged livestock become positives when I want the mowings to compost. My new "livestock" are the microorganisms in the compost heap, and they love wet and dirty hay. This kind of haymaking puts a smile on my face.

♦ Eliot Coleman, *The New Organic Grower*

"The weather looks a little iffy."

KOREN

If compost is the life source of the garden, seeds are the life spark. I have always marveled that a carrot, a bunch of celery, or cabbage could be hidden in such a tiny speck. Yet that small seed is a powerhouse of performance. Take the tomato, for example. Do you want return on investment? One tomato seed, yielding at least 1,000 to 1 in four months, makes even the highest fliers seem paltry. Are you fascinated by design and miniaturization? The finest computer is but a crude makeshift device beside a tomato seed.

◆ Eliot Coleman, *Four-Season Harvest*

"We're presenting this year's award to the tomato—for the way he has deepened our understanding of world conflict resolution, for fostering the ideals of peace, friendship, and international brotherhood, and for being delicious."

Good compost is akin to good wine:
a full body of organic matter, the aroma of sweet
earth, and the taste of all essential nutrients. By
contributing the building blocks from which
microorganisms
renew humus,
compost is the
quintessential
fertilizer.

Michael Phillips, *The Apple Grower*

♦

"Here's to us, kid—and the healing powers of raw juices."

Later Greeks and Romans had a curious belief that, because the herb was a symbol of hostility and insanity, to grow truly fragrant basil one had to shout and swear angrily and outlandishly while sowing its seeds.

♦ Dianne Onstad, *Whole Foods Companion*

"I'm afraid the antipasto is a bit rebellious this evening."

"Everything's fine. The garden is coming in beautifully, and Jeremy is in his usual rage."

If You Can't Beat 'Em—Eat 'Em.

Peter Gail,
The Dandelion Celebration

♦

I remember, as a younger man, the incredible discovery that plant seeds were like temporary resting places— roadside inns on an almost infinite four-dimensional highway. Now I know that bulbs, like garlic, are even more spectacular. They don't pass on their ancient memories— they *are* their ancient memories.

♦ Ron L. Engeland,
Growing Great Garlic

"Kate, this is the wonderful man I told you about who has such a strong hand with garlic and fresh thyme."

An orchard

is much more than
the sum of the
fruit trees growing
within. The soil,
air, sun, and rain
perfect the back-
ground harmony
in which a tiny
cell grows to
become a bud to
become a blossom
to become a
pollinated ovary to
become the
beautiful apple in
your hand.

♦ Michael Phillips,
The Apple Grower

"Mmm, apple pie—an American icon."

In the evening the man stands in his garden and watches the vegetables and thinks:
if this ground of animals to which he belongs had decided,
in an act of selflessness, of generosity and distance from their idea
of themselves, that the supreme act of creativity and intelligence was not to make language
     or history but instead
to make food by photosynthesis,
why, then, this blue-green broccoli here every day more greatly stretching toward the sun
     would be
the ultimate, the pinnacle, the very top
of the pyramid of being!

♦ from "July," David Budbill, *Judevine*

"What's it like to be at the top of the food chain?"

You must learn to think like a flower, to empathize with the flower, to understand the physiological processes that are at work in this small miracle of nature.

♦ Lynn Byczynski, *The Flower Farmer*

"How were you born? Because your Daddy gave some of his pollen to a bee, who gave it to Mommy."

Long before we learned what metaphors were
we had learned that the river was no mere metaphor for life. It was the real thing.
The river brings nourishment and carries away wastes. It bounds and leaps
and cavorts; it is sullen; it plods on; it takes to its heels.
It is the very image of us and our very substance.
Without water there would be no plants,
no animals, no us.

Robert Kimber, *A Canoeist's Sketchbook*

♦

"Honey, are you thinking about the office?"

We once knew a woman who had gardened organically for over two decades. She was forced to move when her husband was transferred to a job some five hundred miles away. She actually had the soil from her garden excavated and moved, in dump trucks, to her new home. That was how much she loved her soil.

♦ Leandre Poisson and Gretchen Vogel Poisson, *Solar Gardening*

"I'm in herbs—celebrating the ancient link between women and plants."

"It's a perfect day to reorganize those closets!"

My advice is to learn to love or at least like worms. They're one of nature's grand cultivators and decomposers. They're quite tame creatures with fascinating habits.

Robert Kourik, in Anne Simon Moffat, Marc Schiler, and the Staff of Green Living, *Energy-Efficient and Environmental Landscaping*

I think of my root cellar as a secret underground garden into which I spirit away many of my crops when winter threatens. The crops don't grow in this garden. They just sit there respiring quietly and looking beautiful. For them, the most delightful place to spend the winter is not some sunny tropical isle but a cold, damp, dark cavern. If that's what they like, that's what I try to provide. It couldn't be easier.

♦ Eliot Coleman, *Four-Season Harvest*

"I'm allergic to the sun."

I am convinced that you must love flowers in order to grow them well. You must have empathy for them and you must be as attentive as a parent. With flowers, familiarity is sure to lead to love.

♦ Lynn Byczynski, *The Flower Farmer*

"Ulrich, that's bad science and you know it!"

To understand a meadow, you really need to sit down in one a while. Maybe like for twenty years.

♦ Gene Logsdon, *The Contrary Farmer*

"<u>Now</u> what?"

"We would do well to read in the woods and fields; to muse in the barn and barnyard; to court familiarity with cows and sheep and swine and hens and haymows . . . that we may infuse something fresh and real into our culture and speech."

John Burroughs, from "Analogy," originally published in *Knickerbocker Magazine* ◆
(December 1862), quoted in Edward J. Renehan, Jr.,
John Burroughs

Plants don't wear out.

Anne Simon Moffat, Marc Schiler,
and the Staff of Green Living,
*Energy-Efficient and Environmental
Landscaping*

♦

"Please—stand by me forever!"

The planting of a tree

is sacred. It matters little that a
hundred or more saplings will go
into the row ahead. Each time we
break open the earth, layer out the
developing roots, and tamp the soil
back in place, we embrace our
mutual destiny with trees.

Michael Phillips,
The Apple Grower

♦

For three years he
had been planting
trees in this
wilderness. He had
planted one hundred
thousand. Of the
hundred thousand,
twenty thousand
had sprouted. Of the
twenty thousand he
still expected to lose
about half, to
rodents or to the
unpredictable
designs of
Providence. There
remained ten
thousand oak trees
to grow where
nothing had grown
before.

Jean Giono, ♦
*The Man Who
Planted Trees*

In my grandfather's day, people celebrated the seasonality and variety of the home garden. They knew that one cabbage tasted best fresh in June and that another made the best sauerkraut. This was the pea for eating fresh and that the one for drying. They were familiar with 50 different apples and 20 pears. They knew when these were ripe and which blended best for cider or complemented the flavor of this or that cheese. We can recover such civilized living again.

♦ Eliot Coleman, *Four-Season Harvest*

"Once upon a time, there was a frozen pizza, and inside the pizza some very bad monsters lived. Their names were refined white flour, reconstituted tomato, and processed cheese. But the worst monster of all was called pepperoni!"

Twenty years and 500,000 cubic yards of moist soil later, I'm still asking myself the same question: Why isn't rammed earth in widespread use? Without doubt it is a lot of work, as are most things of value in life, but the beautiful simplicity of converting raw, natural earth into human habitat involves a sort of sweaty alchemy. If you attempt to build your own rammed earth house, and if the process works as well for you as it has for me, you won't regret the effort.

◆ David Easton, *The Rammed Earth House*

"They're much too permissive."

"The story of Adam and Eve is a beautiful myth. There is an Adam and Eve in Darwin's plan, too, but they were not set up in business on the home-farm, their garden ready planted. They made their own garden, and knew how they came by their acres . . . Grandfather Adam, who ate his steak raw, and Great-Grandfather Adam, who had a tail, and lived in trees, and had a coat of hair."

♦ John Burroughs, journal entry, August 17, 1883, quoted in
Edward J. Renehan, Jr., *John Burroughs*

My garden exists as a part of the natural world, and I pay attention to the patterns of that world. I have a simple rule: if what I am doing in the garden seems complicated, it is probably wrong.

Eliot Coleman, *Four-Season Harvest* ♦

"Next to the laborer in the fields, the walker holds the closest relation to the soil; and he holds a closer and more vital relation to nature." Burroughs proposed walking as a cure for the brash brag and swagger of the stereotypical American. Perhaps the mortal pace of slow, two-legged locomotion would have a humbling effect.

♦ Edward J. Renehan, Jr., *John Burroughs*

"I'd like you to meet Frank Russ. He's just arrived on foot."

Growing apples organically requires a patience measured in years. Observing the intricacies of Nature to find the best approach necessitates the seasons coming round again. And again and again.

♦ Michael Phillips, *The Apple Grower*

Picture the natural world as represented by an embroidered tapestry
hanging from the rafters. The pesticide enthusiasts are all looking at the
back side of the tapestry. From that perspective they see loose ends,
stray threads, and confused patterns. Their science isn't bad,
it's just that they can't see the logic of nature's woven fabric.
They need to step around to the front side.

Eliot Coleman, *The New Organic Grower*

♦

Soil, like an ocean or a forest, is an environment full of lifeforms, both visible and invisible. The life above the ground is a reflection of the life beneath the ground. The health and balance of plant life indicates a health and balance of the same elements in the soil.

◆ Leandre Poisson and Gretchen Vogel Poisson, *Solar Gardening*

"She's the most effective of our emerging new pathogens."

KOREN

I read or heard recently,
I don't remember where:
"A dying man's final words
are unlikely to be 'I wish
I'd watched more TV.'"

Rob Roy, *Mortgage-Free!* ♦

Sunrises and sunsets provide inspiration to artists, lovers, and beach walkers. At the moment of sunset, we instinctively become still. Here is a moment when we can actually look at the Sun, connect with it directly, and share the universe. Words are unnecessary. We are renewed.

♦ Stephen Morris, in John Schaeffer et al., *A Place in the Sun*

"Is this beautiful weather, or what?"

"Could you repeat what you just said? I was on another planet."

It helps to know what hemisphere you live in.

Sim Van der Ryn, architect, in John Schaeffer et al., *A Place in the Sun*

♦

Pests? The systems of the natural world are elegant and logical. The idea of striving to create life-giving foods while simultaneously dousing them with deadly poisons is inelegant and illogical.

♦ Eliot Coleman, *The New Organic Grower*

I realized that only by a continuously deeper and deeper examination of the familiar could I find real meaning in life, and thereby gain some genuine satisfaction from it. I became so excited with this new (to me) realization that I thought my skin was going to rip open.

Gene Logsdon, *The Contrary Farmer's Invitation to Gardening*

Nothing substitutes for
personal knowledge, personal relationship,
and personal responsibility.

Joel Salatin, *Salad Bar Beef*

◆

*"This past summer, I got deeply depressed about our planet—
as if I didn't have enough problems of my own."*

Done. His woodshed full of wood, his little house banked tight
against the cold, the cellar full of meat and vegetables,
he comes inside
and washes blood and summer from his fingernails. In silence now
in the dying year he darkens like the days; he sits and falls
as leaves fall, deeper into the coming dark, into the time of dream.

♦ from "November Again," David Budbill, *Judevine*

Annotated Bibliography

(Unless otherwise indicated, all books are published by Chelsea Green, White River Junction, Vermont)

Berman, Daniel M., and John T. O'Connor. *Who Owns the Sun? People, Politics, and the Struggle for a Solar Economy.* **Foreword by Ralph Nader. 1996**

Narrated against a backdrop of diminishing fossil fuels, environmental degradation, avaricious corporations, and worldwide competition for natural resources, this book shows how existing solar technologies combined with local management present logical remedies for our energy gluttony.

Bryan, Frank, and John McClaughry. *The Vermont Papers: Recreating Democracy on a Human Scale.* **1989.**

Unabashed advocates of such basic American values as self-reliance, tolerance, community aid, diversity, and liberty, the authors argue that democracy is an endangered institution. Bypassed by the Industrial Revolution and buttressed by its tradition of town meeting, Vermont can lead Americans back home, to our roots. *The Vermont Papers* points the way toward a postmodern, human-scale democracy—a sort of Yankee *perestroika*.

Budbill, David. *Judevine.* **1991.**

The setting for *Judevine* happens to be a fictional town in the hills of rural northern Vermont, but it could be any place in America where poverty prevails and where the natural world is still a factor in people's daily lives. David Budbill has been writing his lyrical, dark, funny, narrative poems about the people of Judevine for the past twenty-five years. This is more than a collection of individual poems: *Judevine* becomes one continuous story with the form of an epic poem or a poetic novel.

Byczynski, Lynn. *The Flower Farmer: An Organic Grower's Guide to Raising and Selling Cut Flowers.* 1997.

We don't eat flowers, so why should we grow them organically? The same reasons why organic practices are important for food crops hold for flowers: they protect the health of growers, the people in surrounding communities, the soil, and the environment. "A flower garden should be a place that nourishes your soul."

Byler, Emma (Jonas Em). *Plain & Happy Living: Amish Recipes & Remedies.* Goosefoot Acres Press, 1991.

This little book is full of warm, gentle wisdom and practical suggestions from the veterans of simple living: the old order Amish.

Clark, Sam. *The Real Goods Independent Builder: Designing & Building a House Your Own Way.* 1996.

This is a comprehensive manual of design and building methods for owner-builders as well as professional builders and their clients. In addition to presenting specific techniques, the book explains the design principles and planning processes that underlie all good building, so that readers can develop their own exceptional designs, independently.

Cole, Nancy, and P. J. Skerrett for the Union of Concerned Scientists. *Renewables Are Ready: People Creating Renewable Energy Solutions.* 1995.

Without waiting for politicians and the media to wake up to the economic and environmental benefits of renewable energy, citizens in every part of the United States have taken charge of their own energy destiny. *Renewables Are Ready* documents the renewable energy technologies being put to use in diverse communities across the country.

Coleman, Eliot. *The New Organic Grower: A Master's Manual of Tools and Techniques for the Home and Market Gardener,* revised ed. 1995.

Master grower Eliot Coleman presents the simplest and most sustainable ways to grow top-quality organic vegetables. The book includes extensive practical information on marketing the harvest, on small-scale equipment, and on farming and gardening for the long-term health of the soil.

Coleman, Eliot. *Four-Season Harvest: How to Harvest Fresh, Organic Vegetables from Your Home Garden All Year Long.* 1992.

This book shows how to harvest organically grown vegetables throughout the coldest months in all climate zones with very little extra time or effort. The author's success depends on growing a large variety of vegetables, each suited to their season, and on simple, inexpensive designs for cold frames, unheated mobile greenhouses, and root cellars.

Dobbs, David, and Richard Ober. *The Northern Forest.* 1995.

The authors say they could not write about one of America's last great forests without writing about some of the people who live there. The northern forest—twenty-six million acres stretching across upper New England and New York—is a landscape that has shaped its people as surely as they have shaped the land.

Easton, David. *The Rammed Earth House.* 1996.

An eye-opening example of how the most dramatic innovations in home design and construction frequently have their origins in the distant past. By rediscovering the most ancient of all building materials—earth—forward-thinking home builders can now create structures that set new standards for beauty, durability, and efficient use of natural resources.

Engeland, Ron L. *Growing Great Garlic: The Definitive Guide for Organic Gardeners and Small Farmers.* **Filaree Productions, 1991.**

Written by a small-scale farmer who makes his living growing over two hundred strains of garlic, this book tells when and how to plant, care for, and harvest the crop, as well as how to store, market, and process your garlic.

Gail, Peter. *The Dandelion Celebration: A Guide to Unexpected Cuisine.* **Goosefoot Acres Press, 1990.**

The definitive guide to gathering, preparing, and savoring the entire dandelion, this book will change your attitude toward this most familiar weed.

Giono, Jean. *The Man Who Planted Trees.* **With wood engravings by Michael McCurdy. 1985.**

Jean Giono said the purpose of his story "was to make people love the tree, or more precisely, to make them *love planting trees.*" In this fable, one man of great simplicity and determination works for a lifetime to steadfastly plant one hundred acorns daily, and thus regenerates a ravaged landscape.

Glynn, Thomas. *Hammer. Nail. Wood. The Compulsion to Build.* 1998.

This book is not quite a novel and not quite a construction manual. Glynn infuses his story with the keys—attitude and ingenuity—that really put up a house. He weaves into it the community of humans who live around the house he is building, and the far-flung contemplations that building a house bring to mind.

Hart, Robert. *Forest Gardening: Cultivating an Edible Landscape.* 1996; first published in the U.K. by Green Books, 1991.

Based on the model of a healthy natural woodland, a forest garden incorporates a wide variety of useful plants, including fruit and nut trees, perennial herbs, and vegetables. Blending history, philosophy, anthropology, and seasoned gardening wisdom in a lucid sequence of essays, Hart's book beautifully describes his decades of experience gardening in the Shropshire countryside. Revised and expanded from the English classic with recommended species and resource lists for North America.

Jenkins, Joseph. *The Humanure Handbook: A Guide to Composting Human Manure.* Jenkins Publishing, 1994.

We *know* we shouldn't be flushing it into our drinking water, but what *can* we do with it? Emphasizing minimum technology and maximum hygienic safety, this book takes a humorous approach to the obvious truth that humanure is not waste, it is an agricultural resource.

Jenkins, Joseph. *The Slate Roof Bible: Everything You Wanted to Know About Slate Roofs Including How to Keep Them Alive for Centuries.* Jenkins Publishing, 1997.

Interest in slate roofs is increasing as people recognize their historic value as well as their beauty and practical durability. The author taps into his Welsh ancestry and his thirty years of slate roof restoration experience to provide a detailed and authoritative work, beautifully illustrated and written in layperson's terms.

Kimber, Robert. *A Canoeist's Sketchbook.* 1991.

Part philosopher, part humorist, and an outstanding canoeist, Kimber reveals the heart and soul of the wilderness experience in this alphabetical progression of essays. Along the way, he provides a host of practical tips on how to camp and canoe in remote places.

Levin, Ted. *Blood Brook: A Naturalist's Home Ground.* 1992.

Tracing the course of one small watershed from its source near his home, through a lake and various rivers to the Atlantic Ocean, Levin helps us sharpen our senses and increase our understanding of nature by showing us how one small valley, as a microcosm, entwines with the rest of the biosphere.

Logsdon, Gene. *The Contrary Farmer.* 1994.

Critics of American agriculture bemoan the widespread decline of family farms. Gene Logsdon asserts that the solution to this crisis is cottage farming—farming part-time for fun as well as profit. *The Contrary Farmer* combines the virtues of a manual for the practicing farmer with eloquent meditations in praise of hard work and pleasure.

Logsdon, Gene. *The Contrary Farmer's Invitation to Gardening.* 1997.

The borders of the contrary garden are limited only by the imagination. Why should "crops" be merely common vegetables? Why not wheat? Why not the pigeons on the rafters of the barn, or bluegills and edible cattails from the homestead pond? Frequently irreverent, but always optimistic and practical, Gene Logsdon uses the tools of good humor and common sense to smash conventional gardening to smithereens.

McLure, John. *Baba À Louis Bakery Bread Book: The Secret Book of the Bread.*
Baba À Louis Bakery, 1993.

Baba À Louis Bakery in Proctorsville, Vermont, has offered traditional old-world and
innovative new-style breads to enthusiasts from all over North America for more than
twenty years. Baker John McLure shares his baking techniques and welcomes readers
to the culture of baking, bringing to life the day-to-day routines and pleasures of his
craft in a practical text liberally salted with anecdotes, observations, historical notes,
and quotations.

Meadows, Donella H., Dennis L. Meadows, and Jørgen Randers. *Beyond the
Limits: Confronting Global Collapse, Envisioning a Sustainable Future.* 1992.

Beyond the Limits demonstrates that human use of resources and generation of
pollutants have already exceeded the capacity of the Earth. Yet the book's conclusions
offer us a hopeful choice, a chance to learn to live sustainably. This is not the only
book to make such dire predictions, nor the only one to provide meaningful solutions,
but it is the book to read *first.* Then the smaller, more specific pieces of the puzzle of
how to live in ecological balance will have a context.

Moffat, Anne Simon, Marc Schiler, and the Staff of Green Living. *Energy-
Efficient and Environmental Landscaping.* Appropriate Solutions, 1994.

This book shows how to substantially lower your heating, electric, and water bills, and
make your whole property environmentally friendly.

Nearing, Helen. *Loving and Leaving the Good Life.* 1992.

Helen and Scott Nearing lived together fifty-three years until Scott's death at age one
hundred. This is Helen's memoir of their life together and an inspiring testimonial to
the ideals they stood for: self-sufficiency, simplicity, social justice, and peace.

Onstad, Dianne. *Whole Foods Companion: A Guide for Adventurous Cooks,
Curious Shoppers, & Lovers of Natural Foods.* 1996.

A definitive guide to the rapidly expanding world of whole foods, this book offers
buying tips, culinary uses, health benefits, and nutritional tables, as well as historical
and legendary lore about each food.

Phillips, Michael. *The Apple Grower: A Guide for the Organic Orchardist.* 1998.

The author combines the wisdom and techniques of our great-grandparents' day
for growing apples organically with today's scientific knowledge of pests and
disease cycles to create a readable, comprehensive book with a refreshing
and hopeful philosophy. Phillips doesn't pretend that organic
methods are easy and foolproof; instead, he develops and
promotes an integrated organic method as an alternative to
conventional fruit-growing, for those growers who are
willing to make the commitment.

Poisson, Leandre, and Gretchen Vogel Poisson. *Solar Gardening: Growing Vegetables Year-Round the American Intensive Way.* 1994.

Solar Gardening shows how to increase the effects of the sun during the coldest months of the year and how to protect tender plants from the intensity of the sun during the hottest months through the use of solar "mini-greenhouses."

Potts, Michael. *The Independent Home: Living Well with Power from the Sun, Wind, and Water.* 1993.

Author Michael Potts traveled from Hawaii to Vermont to interview the pioneers of the new, solar lifestyle—families who have learned how to live better by using less energy, many of them completely disconnected from the utility grid.

Renehan, Edward J., Jr. *John Burroughs: An American Naturalist.* 1992.

Writing during the increasingly industrial decades of the late nineteenth and early twentieth centuries, John Burroughs—one of the most popular and preeminent nature writers of his time—stayed constant to the transcendentalist ideal. In this full biography, Edward J. Renehan Jr. draws on a wealth of previously unpublished manuscripts, journals, and letters to reveal the life of the dean of American nature writing.

Roy, Rob. *The Sauna.* 1996.

With a history going back at least one thousand years, the ancient rite of sauna is ready for a new generation of enthusiasts looking for health, pleasure, and peace of mind. The book includes step-by-step instructions for building two styles of sauna, emphasizing the benefits of cordwood masonry construction.

Roy, Rob. *Mortgage-Free! Radical Strategies for Home Ownership.* With illustrations by Malcolm Wells. 1998.

The literal meaning of "mortgage" is "death pledge." Rob Roy offers an escape route from a lifetime of indentured servitude: a complete guide to strategies that allow you to own your land and home, free and clear, without a mortgage.

Salatin, Joel. *Salad Bar Beef.* Polyface, 1995.

In a day when beef is assailed by many environmental organizations, Salatin provides a new paradigm for a socially and ecologically balanced program for a small beef cattle operation. The salad bar beef production model offers hope to rural communities, struggling row-crop farmers, and frustrated beef eaters who do not want to encourage desertification, air and water pollution, environmental degradation, and inhumane animal treatment.

Schaeffer, John, and the Collaborative Design/Construction Team. *A Place in the Sun: The Evolution of the Real Goods Solar Living Center.* 1997.

The Real Goods Solar Living Center, which opened in Hopland, California, in June 1996, embodies the building materials, landscaping techniques, renewable energy technologies, and human design processes that future generations will take for granted. Like the Solar Living Center itself, this book was created by a team of cutting-edge architects, back-to-the-landers from the Mendocino hills, artists, and blue-collar tradespeople.

Schaeffer, John, and the Real Goods Staff. *Real Goods Solar Living Sourcebook: The Complete Guide to Renewable Energy Technologies & Sustainable Living,* 9th ed.

"The bible of independent living and renewable energy."

Schwenke, Karl. *In a Pig's Eye.* 1985.

The author tells stories, sometimes uproarious, sometimes sad, about his encounters with pigs, neighbors, and newcomers in a Vermont town, with a sharp ear for dialogue and for the human qualities of pigs and the pig-like qualities of humans.

Steen, Athena Swentzell, Bill Steen, and David Bainbridge. *The Straw Bale House.* 1994.

This is the book that set off the media frenzy about straw bale houses. And it's not just hype: Whether you build an entire house or something more modest, plastered straw bale construction is an exceptionally durable and inexpensive option. What's more, it's fun, because the technique is easy to learn and easy to do yourself, and the resulting living spaces are unusually quiet, comfortable, and beautiful.

Roulac, John W. *Hemp Horizons: The Comeback of the World's Most Promising Plant.* 1997.

Hemp fiber can replace raw materials such as wood, cotton, and petrochemicals that have higher environmental costs of production, use, and disposal. This book details the immense value of hemp as an agricultural crop, which can generally be grown without pesticides in rotation with other crops, and celebrates hemp's positive impact on rural development, the environment, and sustainable industry.

Taylor, John S. *A Shelter Sketchbook: Timeless Building Solutions.* 1997; originally published as *Commonsense Architecture,* W.W. Norton, 1983.

The traditions of indigenous folk architecture are distinguished by wise use of resources, responsiveness to environmental forces, and a very economical accommodation of human needs. Fortunately, in recent years there has been—for ecological, ethical, and simply pragmatic reasons—a resurgence of interest in buildings that are more respectful of these factors. Through enthralling pen-and-ink sketches, John Taylor depicts and explains more than six hundred elegantly simple and practical structures created by centuries of anonymous builders.

Torjusen, Bente, ed. *Words and Images of Edvard Munch*. 1986.

No longer in print, this book offers a graceful and probing introduction to Munch's art, and to the haunting body of writing he produced over a lifetime.

Van der Ryn, Sim. *The Toilet Papers: Recycling Waste and Conserving Water*. Foreword by Wendell Berry. Ecological Design Press, 1995.

This book provides an informative, inspiring, and irreverent look at how people have dealt with human wastes over the centuries, and at what safe designs are available today that reduce water consumption and avert the necessity for expensive treatment systems.

Weisman, Alan. *Gaviotas: A Village to Reinvent the World*. 1998.

For nearly three decades, the scientists, artisans, rural peasants, ex-urban street kids, and Guahibo Indians living in the Colombian village called Gaviotas have elevated phrases like "sustainable development" and "appropriate technology" from cliché to reality. Yet human beings and their technology are not the only heroes. In the shelter of millions of Caribbean pines, which the Gaviotans planted as a renewable crop, a miracle has occurred: the regeneration of an ancient native rain forest. The story of Gaviotas, a village alchemizing peace and prosperity in a stricken land, will change the way you think of the world.

Zelov, Chris, and Phil Cousineau, eds. *Design Outlaws on the Ecological Frontier*. Knossus Publishers, 1997.

A companion to the award-winning film *Ecological Design: Inventing the Future,* this book gathers together interviews of more than twenty of the leading designers and architects who have followed in the footsteps of Buckminster Fuller—and then made their own paths.

◆

A limited number of 18" x 24" color posters with the cartoon art from the cover of *The Hard Work of Simple Living* are available from Chelsea Green:

Glossy stock	$12.95
Hemp/recycled stock *signed by Ed Koren*	$35.00

To order, call (800) 639-4099.

What is a Sustainable Hedonist?

- ♦ *A sustainable hedonist is an electric guitarist with a solar-powered amplifier.*

- ♦ *A sustainable hedonist fills the hot tub with condensate captured above the maple sugaring pans.*

- ♦ *Sustainable hedonists eat when they're hungry, sleep when they're tired, and burst into song at unexpected moments.*

Now that you've had a chance to read the quotations and enjoy the cartoons in this book, and have begun to fill the blank portions of the pages with your own musings, we would like to know your response to this question. Send your answers to:

Chelsea Green Publishing Company
P.O. Box 428
White River Junction, Vermont 05001
FAX: (802) 295-6444
www.chelseagreen.com

We will publish some of the most interesting or amusing responses in the next issue of our newsletter, *The Junction*. If we use yours, we'll send you a really nifty prize.

Library of Congress Cataloging-in-Publication Data
Koren, Edward.
The hard work of simple living : a somewhat blank book for the
sustainable hedonist / artwork by Edward Koren : with contributions
from the invisible universe.
    p.   cm.
Includes bibliographical references.
ISBN 1-890132-13-6 (alk. paper)
1. Quality of life—Caricatures and cartoons. 2. American wit and
    humor, Pictorial.   I. Title
    NC1429.K62A4   1998
    741.5'973—dc21   98-20538